FM

the first three hundred years

Fresh dainties are by Britain's traffic known,
And now by constant Use familiar grown;
What Lord of old would bid his Cook prepare
Mangoes, Botargo, Champignons, Caviare?

Dr William King, *The Art of Cookery* 1705

Introduction

Everyone remembers their first encounter with Fortnum & Mason. Multiply that by 300 years at the very heart of things and it's clear that we could write a rather longer book than this. Instead we thought it best to cover some of our own favourite memories.

After all, being 300 years young is no excuse for a dry history lesson. Those selling food are more conscious than most of the need to keep things fresh, so what we have here is an enlightening glimpse at the things that still make us tick as lustily as our famous clock.

Unlike our timepiece, we're not bound by chronology. You may find a snippet from WW2 nestling against Napoleon, or Henry Heinz beside Charles Dickens. Stranger things have happened at Fortnum's over the years.

And, in these days of extreme this, that and the next thing, we realise that what we have been up to all this time is Extreme Shopkeeping. How agreeable to be able finally to put a name to it.

Now, gentle reader, step inside to have your senses stretched. In the most delightful way, of course.

Taking the Centuries in our Stride

Fortnum & Mason was established in 1707 and grows more fabulous every year

1707   1807   1907   2007

Mr Fortnum meeting Mr Mason

Fortnum, meet Mason

1707 saw at least two momentous events: the founding of Fortnum & Mason and... what was it? Oh yes. The invention of Great Britain. The Act of Union with Scotland placed Englishness at the top of every agenda, while William Fortnum's name joined Mr Mason's above a brand new grocer's shop that would come to define the essence of Englishness as well as a Cropwell Bishop Stilton or Gloucester Old Spot Pie.

The Age of Enlightenment

Like all great exercises in creation, Fortnum & Mason began with light. The insistence of Queen Anne's household on fresh candles every night spelled a legitimate perk for an enterprising footman: spare palace wax to sell on. By 1707, William Fortnum's enlightened sideline had melted down into enough to leave royal service and start a business with his landlord Hugh Mason. The rest, as they say, is grocery.

First row left: Toiletries, 2nd Floor *First row right:* The Tea Department, Ground Floor
Second row left: Fresh Produce, Lower Ground Floor *Second row right:* The Lingerie Department,
2nd Floor *Third row left:* The Atrium *Third row right:* Exclusive Perfumes,
2nd Floor *Fourth row left:* Choosing the Right Cheeses, Lower Ground Floor
Fourth row right: A selection of Fine Wines, Lower Ground Floor

1707 Wine Bar

181 Piccadilly

Though Fortnum & Mason has been active on the site since 1707 (and Hugh Mason's stables for rather longer), the building itself isn't as old as all that. While based on the Italianate design of the early Victorian period it actually dates from 1926-1930, when the London County Council was refurbishing the whole of Piccadilly. Four years and half a million pounds were what it took to turn London's premier high-class grocery emporium into a magnificent department store like no other.

2007 will see the store's next great emergence, after a top-to-toe refurbishment that cost rather more than half a million pounds. A new Fresh Food Hall, a Wine Bar that was winning awards from the moment it opened, four magnificent restaurants, a central lightwell and atrium, a… we could go on. It may be better just to come and marvel for yourself.

Luring Anatolian lions with Turkish Delight

From Anne to the Georges

If we believe our own world changes fast, imagine living at a time when whole new continents were there to be stumbled upon. Society was sprinting to keep pace and London, especially the new "West End", was in the vanguard.

As the grander houses began to be lit beyond daylight hours the evening meal became all the rage, fashionably featuring the fascinating fare fetching up daily at the docks.

This entirely new phenomenon called for an entirely new species of enterprise. Fortnum's shed light on everything – including society. Its close relations with the East India Company democratised access to the world's supplies and suddenly everything was as clear as day: if you required tea, coffee, cocoa, spices or anything similarly new-fangled, no-one could hold a candle to Fortnum's.

Sweet acorn –
appreciating itself

Salmon –
Bobbed and smoked

Shad's Roe –
Taking to the bottle

*The Spanish
Olive*

The Madness of King George

Charles Fortnum, grandson of the original William, remained in royal service to King George III and Queen Charlotte. As the monarch's mental state declined Charles found his role increasingly challenging and in 1788 left to concentrate on the business, an event noted in Alan Bennett's screenplay: "to Piccadilly, sire, to start a grocer's shop".

Chronological licence aside, he might have found comfort in contemplating that at least he was on the right side of the channel: the French Revolution was *un petit an* away.

LOTS TO SEE
and PLENTY OF LIFTS!

4TH FLOOR

Christmas Cards
Children's Clothes
Stationery

3RD FLOOR

Miss Wethered
Sports and Games
Overseas and other
Equipment
Men's Outfitting & Tailoring
En Tout Cas

2ND FLOOR

Ladies' Shoes and Stockings
Furnishing, Fabrics and Furniture
Lamps and Lampshades
Household Linens

1ST FLOOR

Ladies' Sportswear, Hats,
Model Room, Furs,
Perfumery, Lingerie, Gloves
Ready to Wear

GROUND FLOOR

Good Things to Eat
Chocolates, Cakes, Wines,
Cigars, Fruit, Flowers
and the Restaurant

LR GROUND FLOOR

The loveliest Gift
Department you ever saw

Colonel Wyld's Vision

Charles Wyld joined the company in 1905 as Managing Director, direct from the Coldstream Guards. He had great plans for the expansion of the business and, to that end, began to buy up the leases of adjoining properties. The Great War halted this progress but in 1926 he saw his moment and seized the day. What was his store like? Let's take a tour.

The ground and mezzanine floors remained dedicated to gastronomic delights, with a restaurant serving delicious light meals made in the famous Fortnum kitchens. Visitors could see the rose & violet creams being made by hand on the premises, and the wine department was happy to store customers' cellars (and cigars) at no extra charge.

Ladies' fashions, from shoes and gloves to evening dresses and sportswear, were serviced by a workroom full of experienced seamstresses. Children could play on a giant carousel while their mothers chose haute couture clothes for them.

Fortnum's customers in *Harpers Magazine*, 1933. *Left:* Design for cruising, in navy blue and white – Mrs Dennis Cohen; *Centre:* Spring green & white – Mrs Philip Kindersley; *Right:* A frock for the beach, the garden or the tennis court – The Duchess of Laurino

Top: Harold Knights' portrait of Colonel Wyld, commissioned and presented by the staff of Fortnum's in 1935
Left: Lots to See and Plenty of Lifts, 1934

Anyone for a Tennis Court?

Men had a floor to themselves, where they could not only be measured for a suit but shop for stationery, indoor games or that tiresomely regular essential, a new tennis court. We're here to serve.

Open Sesame

By 1934, the fourth floor was an Aladdin's cave of the most beautifully staged rooms, each displaying the skills of the interior design, furniture and antiques department. Here also were held the exhibitions showcasing new artists from across the Empire. At the very top of the building was the Tropical Equipment and Expeditions Department, where the adventurous could find everything they wished (down to the last chop box) for that safari or quest for rare Himalayan plants.

The Jermyn Street frontage remained the favoured spot for temporary departments (most notably the famous Christmas Cracker Shop) until the 1950s, when a new institution – the Fountain Restaurant – opened to great acclaim. The interior design service gave way to an enlarged Antiques Department and a fourth floor restaurant that is still a haven of good food, impeccable service and tranquillity today.

Fortnum & Mason's Private Golosh Park

First row left: Pastry Chefs, 1960 *First row right:* The Tea Counter, 1990
Second row left: The Model Room, 1955 *Second row right:* Children's Carousel, 1970s
Third row left: Service Staff in the Fountain Restaurant, 1955 *Third row right:* The Wine Crypt, 1957
Fourth row left: The Provisions Counter, 1980 *Fourth row right:* Personal Service, 1957

Our Hourly Outing

Having only been there since 1964, our clock is something of a whippersnapper. Yes, those figures of our founders aren't actually taken from life. After the company's 250th anniversary celebrations the management decided to give London a new landmark, something that would grace that most elegant of thoroughfares. On 4th November 1964, at high noon, this ornament to Piccadilly was unveiled. It had taken three years to build. It was worth the wait.

Four-foot high figures of Mr Fortnum and Mr Mason appear on the hour. Mr Fortnum is the one with the tea tray while Mr Mason holds a branched candelabra. As the clock begins to chime, they move forward to the edge of their platforms, turn towards each other and bow. In all these years they've never once bumped heads. Once the clock has chimed the hour, a series of airs is played on eighteen bells. As the tune ends, Mr Fortnum and Mr Mason bow once more to each other and move back into their pavilions. What they talk about for the next 58 minutes is anyone's guess.

It was part of the brief that only the best firms be used in the construction of the clock and, to this end, artisans from companies even older than Fortnum & Mason were used. The bell founders were Mears and Stainbank, who can trace their origins back to the reign of Queen Elizabeth 1 and whose canon of work includes Great Tom at Oxford, Big Ben and the Bow Bells. At over four tons in weight, erection of the clock required major structural work on the building. Such was the interest that a viewing window was created on the Second Floor, which then housed the Ladies' Fashion Department. The clock has become part of the London landscape. More tunes have been added and plenty of Piccadilly pedestrians pause patiently to partake of carols at Christmas or 'Happy Birthday' on the sovereign's official birthday.

Fortnum's Famous Windows

What is a shop: a mere place to buy things, or a window on the world? Fortnum's has always been the latter, and for decades its actual casements have hosted an ever-changing display of quite breathtaking invention. To call each display a work of art is to damn with faint praise: these are miniature museums, hymns to the seasons, captive carnivals of creativity whose every unveiling energises Piccadilly anew.

A Fortnum's window display is not there to alert you to reductions in refrigerators or how much one might care to spend on trousers. Rather it remains defiantly artistic, its aim to inspire and enthral. As our current chief designer has it, each is "a gift to our customers." Or, to quote his fabled predecessor, "the glass represents the division between the real world and the unlimited realm of fantasy".

If they make you feel that Fortnum's is the fountain of the fabulous, they're more than earning their keep.

Created by Chris Blackwell, Design Director from 1973 to 2006 *Left:* Food and wine being displayed on an imposing Renaissance credenza *Right:* On delicate pink tulip petals boxes of luxurious and exculsive chocolates are surrounded by silvery sugared almonds

The Composer of our Derby hamper menus hibernating in the Bayeux Tapestry of our Inner Temple during the Steeplechasing season

Fortnum & Hampers

To some, Fortnum's more or less equates to hampers: sent perhaps by an appreciative colleague, client or house guest once or twice a year. Just think what they are missing! Although we have to say it's understandable, as we more or less invented the idea of packing them full of portable provisions to a standard not before seen (and certainly not available in every coaching inn on the way to one's country pile).

Piccadilly (or Portugal Street) was hard to avoid, especially when travelling westwards. It made a logical place to take on provisions and a Fortnum's hamper made the logical vessel. Aside from a favourable strength/weight equation, one of the great advantages of the wicker basket was its ability, before the term was ever coined, to be recycled. Before long it became a badge of knowing one's portable onions, and before our first centenary the idea had really taken off.

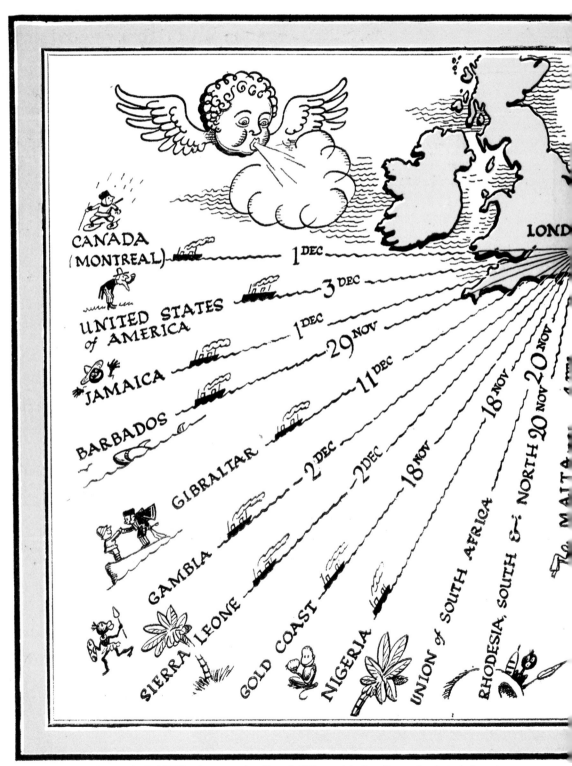

CANADA (MONTREAL) — 1 DEC

UNITED STATES of AMERICA — 3 DEC

JAMAICA — 1 DEC

BARBADOS — 29 NOV

GIBRALTAR — 11 DEC

GAMBIA — 2 DEC

SIERRA LEONE — 2 DEC

GOLD COAST — 18 NOV

NIGERIA — 18 NOV

UNION of SOUTH AFRICA — 18 NOV

RHODESIA, SOUTH & NORTH — 20 NOV

LOND[ON]

20 NOV

MALT[A]

Christmas delivery service for 1931. The observant reader will note in 1931, any celebration of human diversity tended towards the sterotypical. How very glad we are that things have moved along

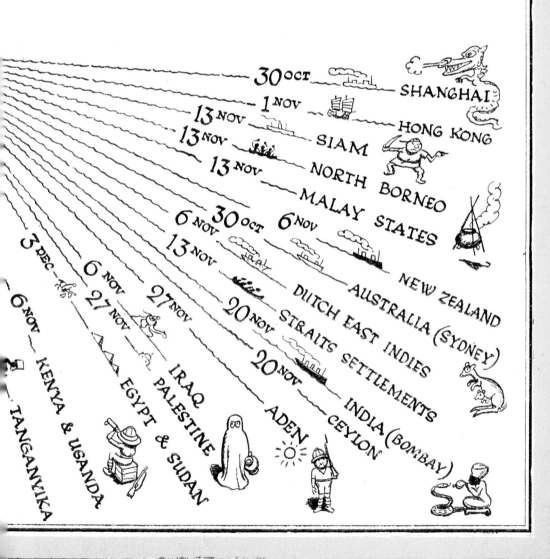

S MAP SHOWS YOU THE APPROXIMATE

TES OF POSTING CHRISTMAS PARCELS

M LONDON TO PLACES OVERSEAS——

30 OCT — SHANGHAI
1 NOV — HONG KONG
13 NOV — SIAM
13 NOV — NORTH BORNEO
13 NOV — MALAY STATES
30 OCT — 6 NOV — NEW ZEALAND
6 NOV — AUSTRALIA (SYDNEY)
13 NOV — DUTCH EAST INDIES
20 NOV — STRAITS SETTLEMENTS
20 NOV — INDIA (BOMBAY)
CEYLON
ADEN
27 NOV — IRAQ
27 NOV — PALESTINE
6 NOV — EGYPT & SUDAN
3 DEC
6 NOV — KENYA & UGANDA
TANGANYIKA

Hamper Vincit Omnia

Driven by the passion of Prince Albert, the Great Exhibition of 1851 was London's tribute to the Industrial Revolution. Fortnum & Mason won first prize as *importers of dried fruits and dessert goods* but their influence on the nation's habits was by then acknowledged to be far greater.

Pre-fabrication was all the rage: the Exhibition's home, Crystal Palace, was manufactured in a factory and then assembled on site, and Fortnum's led a similar trend in ready-to-eat luxury foods such as "poultry and game in aspic, hard-boiled eggs in forcemeat (the famous "Scottish egg"), dry and green turtle, boar's head, truffles, mangoes... all decorated and prepared so as to require no cutting."

Charles Dickens wrote of one Epsom Derby;

"Look where I will.... I see Fortnum & Mason. All the hampers fly wide open and the green downs burst into a blossom of lobster salad!"

Charles Dickens

Similar references in Henry James, Wilkie Collins and others – and the preponderance of our hampers at Ascot, the Boat Race, Henley, Wimbledon and Lord's - by the middle of its second century meant that Fortnum's had become *the* out-of-household name.

THE TIMBER DRAG.—A NEW SENSATION FOR THE DERBY.

Derby Day

Alas, not all hampers reached their destination, as witnessed by the fate of one taken in a carriage by social climbers to the races during the 1880s. *"...So lost were they in their conviviality that they dropped the hamper from the carriage, and were not aware of the fact until too late. It's an ill wind that blows nobody any good, however, so the party of ragamuffins [hanging on behind] thought who discovered it, and who at once turned into a churchyard to enjoy the good things accidentally provided for them."*

Fortnum's Celebrated Catalogues

From the mid-nineteenth century far-flung customers were kept informed of what was new and exciting at Fortnum's by means of regular catalogues. Until the early 1920s these were rather matter-of-fact publications, respectfully informing customers of the goods for sale but not always of the prices. If one had to ask…

1924 changed all that forever when Managing Director Colonel Wyld engaged an advertising man of genius called Hugh Stuart Menzies to create a unique form of commercial catalogue. The world had changed much since 1914. Many of the large houses in St. James's had been demolished, turned into offices or divided into flats. After the war the young women destined to inherit their parents' or husbands' accounts might never marry. Fortnum & Mason had to reach a new audience while persuading old friends to continue their patronage. The result of the necessity to survive into this brave new world was two-fold: a new building on the historic site and a venture into advertising that took the capital by storm.

The catalogues were so distinctive that they merited a whole page spoof in Punch. Fortnum & Mason was so delighted with this acclaim that they had the page reprinted and dispatched to their customers. The Commentaries and specialist catalogues continued throughout the 1920s and 1930s with new artists being engaged, including Rex Whistler and Edward Bawden. Whistler's designs for Christmas catalogue covers, and his vibrant drawings for home entertaining and overseas catalogues, were a huge hit with customers, as were Bawden's modernist (and futuristic) designs. Catalogues for shooting parties in Scotland, for American groceries, for shoes, for art exhibitions, tea, perfumery, children's clothes, Christmas crackers, indoor games and outdoor sports all highlighted the ever-more surprising store that was Fortnum & Mason and the delights that were available in-store and by mail order.

Cocktail parties that rise to new heights

Christmas catalogue covers. Can you spot the Rex Whistler and Edward Bawden covers?

1924

1927

1929

1931

1932

1933

1934

1937

1938

1940

1947

1948

1949

1950

1951

1952

1953

1954

1955

1956

1957

1958

1959

1960

1962

American Groceries

Fortnum & Mason Ltd.

181 Piccadilly, London, W.1

REGent 8040

Winsom Ideas for your Country Stores Edward Bawden; *Everything for Cocktails and Cocktail Parties* Edward Bawden; *Wines & Cigars* Ruth Gill; *Invalid Delicacies Simply Encourgage Malingering* W.M. Hendy; *Don't forget your Friends Overseas* W.M. Hendy; *Ices* Rex Whistler

True English Gentleman rescuing the beautiful blonde ham
from the naughty Bath Chap

Blonde and Brunette Hams

THE PEER had eaten beneath him—some youthful folly
with a common imported ham that had led him to the
brink of ruin. "I've done with hams," he said, grinding
his teeth, "now I take my pleasure where I find it—
in Corner Houses—anywhere." We introduced him
to a couple of our well-born hams—a brunette and a blonde.
The Bradenham brunette, almost Spanish in the passionate
beauty of her swarthy treacle cure, the blonde an exquisite
contrast of Suffolk sugar cure—like a wild rose in her gentle
English naïveté. "With either at your breakfast table for
keeps life would pass in sweet rhythm," we said, and as we
stole away we saw his lordship advance and imprint a timid
kiss upon the blonde

Bradenham Treacle-cured Hams 2/6 a lb
Suffolk Sugar-cured Hams   2/6 ,,

REEL
3

The F&M Commentaries

A Manx cow taunting a tin of Oxtail Soup

Fortnum & Mason produced a series of 'Commentaries' that took a different (but current) theme. A military tattoo, cinema stars, the Royal Academy Summer Exhibition, fox-hunting: all became the focus of a light-hearted, cartoon-infused catalogue. Goods for sale were mentioned by-the-by but that was not the point of the publications. They were intended to make readers smile, to recall just what a delightful experience shopping with Fortnum's was, and how the goods they sold could brighten the gloomiest day. Fortnum & Mason did not pretend to sell necessities at rock-bottom prices. It proudly revelled in its rôle as providers of 'dainties'; the little things that make life fun. The catalogues were an immediate success, garnering praise from that old misanthrope, George Bernard Shaw, and approbation from the professional advertising press: worth quoting in full, we feel.

"Every once in so often there drops out of the advertising sky a little manna to gladden the heart and feast the soul of weary travellers in the wilderness of direct mail literature. Just such a heavenly offering is a little sixteen-page booklet issued by Fortnum & Mason of 182 Piccadilly, London, in which turtle soup, game patties and other such delicacies are described in language so savory as to delight the gourmet and tempt the abstinent. This little book puts to shame the lacklustre efforts of most cataloguers and price-listers. What mortal with his gastronomical apparatus in proper functioning order could resist the appeal made on behalf of caviare, as eaten by mermaids in cool grottos? No hackneyed or stock phrases...but language apt and gracious; an aristocracy of expression that makes commonplace words glitter and sparkle with prismatic brilliancy...In so simple a thing as tabulation of what may be had for "one little guinea", the copywriter's genius, inspired by an epicurean appreciation of rare viands, shines forth...no talk of calories or vitamins in this jewel of a booklet, but esoteric phrases contrived to titillate the taste buds and excite the salivary glands; a happy disposition of words, wrought with an indefinable charm that must bring a chuckle from the heart of the most dyspeptic while it wrings a tear of regret from his eye. And the illustrations! Pen and ink drawings by an artist who took seriousness by the scruff of the neck and threw it out of his studio window. The result is a perfect specimen of direct-mail literature in which the art work and typographic treatment mirror the spirit of the copy." The Advertising and Selling Fortnightly, 3 December 1924.

Bolshie Lobster attempting to Belt an Earl

Commentary on
D·A·I·N·T·I·E·S
to fit you for the
Stress of Autumn

WRITTEN AND PREPARED BY FORTNUM AND MASON

Instructions for use of Commentary
Guaranteed free from colouring
matter or unappearance of any kind. Highly
recommended by nursing mothers
after being well shaken

182 Piccadilly W1   Phone Regent 0040

Imitation Cheddar up to its tricks

HERE'S
FORTNUM & MASON'S
EASTER
COMMENTARY
AND IT'S
FUNNIER THAN EVER

This is the
WILLOW PATTERN
*COMM*E*NTARY*

"All the world's a plate
and all the dishes Fortnum and Mason's"
From adaptation from As You Like It
Act 2, Scene VII

Issued by FORTNUM AND MASON in their
Fine Old Georgian House *at* 182 PICCADILLY W1

FORTNUM & MASON'S
GREAT
EASTER FILM DRAMA
ENTITLED
Ravishing Dainties

Blonde Suffolk Ham being misled by a heartless Bath Chap

Released from 182 PICCADILLY, *London*
BOX OFFICE TELEPHONE FOR ORDERS · REGENT 8040

¶ King John solacing
himself with our
pressed beef after
Runnymede

DAINTIES
of the *Utmost Ravishment*
FORTNUM & MASON

this Nineteenth COMMENTARY *is illustrated
from Morsels of Tapestry still adhering to
to our venerable structure at*
182 PICCADILLY

Arrival of the Cos Lettuce Season
AFTER ROSSETTI

Sublime Thoughts on
Eating *and* Drinking
embellished with
MASTERPIECES

*And issued with Proud Humility by Fortnum & Mason
at their Zenith at 182 Piccadilly
This being the 20th Commentary*

The 22nd of the
Commentaries

Fortnum & Mason
hatching the
Easter Egg

Fortnum & Mason's
EASTER
COMM*ENTARY*
DESCRIBES
DAINTIES
BEFORE THE CHARMS OF WHICH
Brave Men Crash

ISSUED AFTER WINE
from 182 PICCADILLY

LORD OF THE
ADMIRALTY TURNING TURTLE
(owing to treachery with his Plimsoll line)

DAINTIES
THAT FIT YOU TO
**span the winter
at one bound**

This is the **SEAFARING** number of FORTNUM AND
MASON'S **COMMENTARY** issued from their
ENHANCED PREMISES 182 Piccadilly

FRANS HALS POURING OIL ON TROUBLED WAITER

Fortnum & Mason's
DUTCH ART
COMMENTARY
Easter 1929

Illustrated by OLD MASTERS from Over the Way and issued from
182 PICCADILLY. This being the 24th literal Commentary

Our Provision Manager has had a baby Stilton

Fortnum & Mason's
30th COMMENTARY
· is written to ·
create
CRAVING

Issued with their usual élan by FORTNUM AND MASON of 182 Piccadilly, W1
and 697 Madison Avenue, New York

OCTOBER 1951

The day we forgot to leave our van at home

Let Us Gallop Furiously
for this is the
HUNTING NUMBER
of
FORTNUM AND MASON'S COMMENTARY
on
DAINTIES THAT INSPIRE RECKLESS DARING

The MEET will be at 182 PICCADILLY

Would-be Premier who counted his Caviar before it was hatched

Fortnum & Mason's
votive
COMMENTARY
deals with
DAINTIES
to maintain your
constitution

Written in a political passion and issued without a second thought from 182 PICCADILLY

FORTNUM & MASON'S COMMENTARY

Notables leaving Grosvenor Square for the Country

THIS NUMBER DEALS WITH
Good Things for Picnics
and other occasions
AND IS ENTITLED
"LET US GO TO THE COUNTRY"
OUR SHOP
is the 182nd House in PICCADILLY

Telephone: REGENT 41

THE PARK

Sampler Number
OF
FORTNUM
& MASON'S
Commentary
182 PICCADILLY
London, West One

FORTNUM & MASON
call this their
Military Tattoo
Commentary
BECAUSE
IT DEALS WITH
FOOD
worth Fighting for

Screened and produced during an access of Martial fervour at
182 PICCADILLY
LONDON
THE FOURTEENTH OF THE SERIES

Fortnum & Mason's Mounted Guards defying the lightning

BALLET!

Egging on Easter

JOYOUS DAINTIES
for
Easter Eating

This, the 18th Commentary
issued by Fortnum & Mason
is entitled
Advertising
Without Tears
182 Piccadilly

Our *Chef*, our *Secretary*, and our *Crystallized Fruit Expert*
entreat you to ORDER *EARLY* before Xmas. It will save
Us many a *back-ache*

A COMMENTARY *on the*
THINGS YOU CRAVE FOR
IN WINTER-TIME
when discretion demands *high-living*
and CERTAIN LUXURIES with which to
combat *THE COLD VAPOURS*

Published in fair and legible characters by
FORTNUM *and* MASON
well settled at 182 PICCADILLY, W1
for the last 214 years or so

November 1924: This being the *7th Commentary* of the series

Our hen putting her best foot foremost
for Easter

the Easter
COMMENTARY
of FORTNUM & MASON
182 PICCADILLY · LONDON

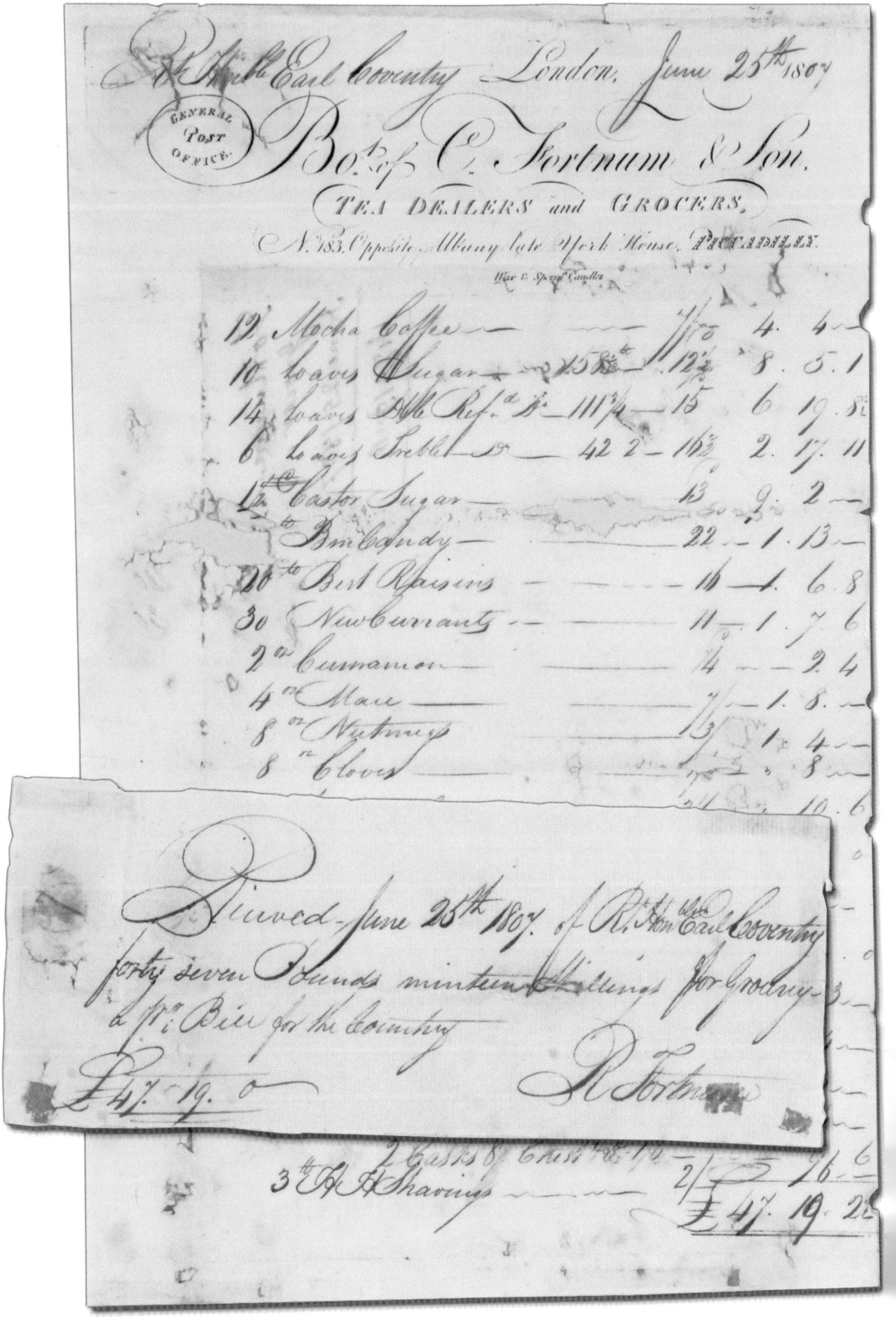

Rt Honble Earl Coventry   London, June 25th 1807

Bot of C. Fortnum & Son.

TEA DEALERS and GROCERS,

No. 183. Opposite Albany, late York House. PICCADILLY.

Wax & Spermaceti Candles

			£	s	d
12 lb	Mocha Coffee	7/6	4	4	—
10	Loaves Sugar — 158 lb	12½	8	5	1
14	Loaves Dble Refd Do — 111½	15	6	19	5½
6	Loaves Treble Do — 42 2	16¾	2	17	11
14 lb	Castor Sugar	13	—	9	2
	to Bm Candy	22	—	1	13
20 lb	to Best Raisins	16	—	1	6	8
30	New Currants	11	—	1	7	6
2 oz	Cinnamon	4	—	—	2	4
4 oz	Mace	7/	—	1	8
8 oz	Nutmegs	13	1	4	—
8 oz	Cloves	7/5	—	5	8
			24	10	6

Received June 25th 1807 of Rt Honble Earl Coventry
forty seven Pounds nineteen Shillings for Grocery
& Wax Bill for the Country

£47. 19. 0   R Fortnum

	2 Casks & Chest &c	2/	26	6
3 lb H H Shavings				
			£47. 19. 2½

Fortnum's horse-drawn van delivering hampers

Fortnum's Delivered

"No item too small, no destination too far." As a promise, it's not exactly cryptic. While the goods on our shelves have always spanned the globe, Fortnum's customers have too. The company has done its utmost to service that demand.

Personal shoppers have never made up the majority. From our earliest days an army of young messengers dressed in Fortnum & Mason livery would call at the kitchen door of the great West End houses taking orders and making small deliveries. Larger orders might merit the distinctive Fortnum & Mason horse-drawn van, while in the late early Victorian era the new railways allowed same-day delivery of postal and, soon, telegraphed and telephonic orders to the local railway station. Whether it was sending a regular store cupboard order to Wales or sending provisions to shooting parties in Scotland by the night express, no delivery was too difficult.

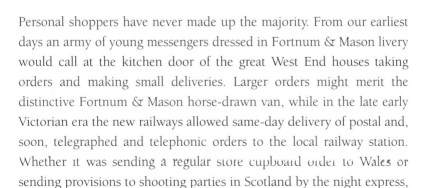

Waterloo to Anywhere

The foremost establishment in a country derided by Napoleon as a "nation of shopkeepers," Fortnum & Mason helped the British army march on its stomach to final victory over *Le Petit Corsican*.

A redcoat officer was expected to provide his own victuals, so it's no wonder the army was among the first to exploit Fortnum's international service. During the Napoleonic Wars a stream of pleading correspondence found its way to 181 Piccadilly: 'I beg you to send me out hams, tongues, butter and cheese..."

The firm duly delivered such supplies to a continent at war but eventually had to send the goods out in unmarked crates, as the distinctive "F&M" alerted sailors and stevedores to the contents, and much went missing *en route* to the awaiting adjutants.

Heartfelt Thanks from Other Ranks

Fortnum & Mason not only delivered regular orders to army officers but was one of the firms commissioned by *The Times* appeal to send goods to ordinary soldiers whose plight had been highlighted by the newspaper's war correspondent. One lucky recipient wrote to his sister:

Balaklava, Jan. 19th

My dearest Alice,

I have just received a box from Fortnum & Mason's, which left that delicious shop I believe in July — pretty management on the part of somebody — however it is just as good as the day it started — nothing the least injured, & the Compton cheese in beautiful order.

Victoria, Beef Tea
& Florence Nightingale

In 1854 the story of the Charge of the Light Brigade gripped the nation. The Crimean was the first war to be covered by on-the-spot reporters, so for once the home front was aware of the soldiers' appalling conditions.

The Queen took a personal interest, sending Fortnum's an order "to dispatch without delay to Miss Nightingale in Scutari" a huge consignment of concentrated beef tea, after the scandal of the hospitals had become known in England.

Every ship that sailed for the Crimea carried cases labelled Fortnum & Mason. Once again many officers wrote begging us to leave it off to discourage pilferers – by now an epidemic, sparked by the sight of our name.

WWI

The experience of two centuries came to the fore during the Great War as officers of all services relied on Fortnum & Mason to supplement their rations. Fortnum & Mason ran many officers' messes in Britain and in France while families could send 'service boxes' full of tinned, dried and bottled foodstuffs to the Western Front and in Mesopotamia, via agents as far flung as Alexandria, Malta and Salonika. The Red Cross licensed the company to send supplies to prisoners of war, so capture did not preclude the unfortunate serviceman from enjoying the delights of home. By 1915, demand for an increase in service was such that an Officers' Supplies Department was opened at Piccadilly, selling everything from uniforms to tents, inflatable baths, hurricane lamps and water-resistant matches. As for sending food to the trenches, we soon learned that only metal tins were any use against the ever-present gourmet rats.

The Home Front

In the Great War all Fortnum's staff serving in France and Flanders were guaranteed to have kept their jobs on their return – which a surprising number managed. In the meantime, the women of London kept things buzzing along quite brilliantly.

Delicacies and essentials
for the first Christmas at the front, 1914

BOXES & PARCELS FOR POST

"SOVEREIGN" BOX No. 1

2 Boxes Chocolate Rations	1 ½-lb Tin Mayfort Tobacco
1 Tin Acid Drops	1 Tin, 50 Cigarettes, Grand Format
1 Tin Cake	
1 Skin Beef Tea	1 Housewife
2 Tins Potted Meats	1 Pocket Handkerchief
1 Tablet Carbolic Soap	1 Tooth Brush
1 Tube Vaseline, Carbolated	1 Pair Porpoise Boot-laces

Packing and Postage included . . **Price £1 . 0 . 0**

"SOVEREIGN" BOX No. 2

1 Tin F & M's Chocolate Rations	1 Tin Sardines
2 ,, F & M's Potted Meats	1 ,, Condensed Milk
1 Tin ,, F & M's Acid Drops	1 ,, Cocoa and Milk
1 ,, F & M's Peppermint Lozenges	1 ,, F & M's Marmalade
	1 ,, Dorset Butter
1 Skin F & M's Beef Tea	1 ,, Cheddar Cheese
1 Tin F & M's Meat Lozenges	1 Fruit Cake
1 ,, F & M's Sausages	1 F & M's Plum Pudding

Packing and Postage included . . **Price £1 . 0 . 0**

BOXES & PARCELS

PARCELS POST BOX

1 Khaki Flannel Shirt	1 Elect[ric]
1 Pair Woollen Socks	1 Extra
1 Housewife	1 Pair [M]

Packing and Postage included .

PARCELS POST BOX

25 Ramon Allones Cigars	½-lb M[ayfort]
100 Grand Format Cigarettes	1 Pipe

Packing and Postage included .

PARCELS POST BO[X]

25 Romeo and Juliette Cigars	1 Tin
1 Tin F & M Plum Pudding	1 Tin
2 Tins ,, Potted Meats	
1 Tin F & M Stilton Cheese	1 Pair

Packing and Postage included . .

CIGARS, CIGARETTES AND TOBACCO

BY PARCELS POST

FREE OF ENGLISH AND FRENCH DUTY

CIGARETTES

Minimum quantity 200.

	Per 100		Per 100
[Su]perfine No. 3—Special Turkish . .	5/-	Special Turkish—Medium size .	4/-
[G]rand Format—Egyptian Blend .	4/-	Special Turkish—Small size .	3/-
Virginia No. 1 .	4/- per 100		

Postage on 200 Cigarettes	.	.	1/-
,, 500 ,,	.	.	1/4
,, 1,000 ,,	.	.	1/7

CIGARS

BY PARCELS POST

[Bri]tish made from Havana Tobacco. Minimum quantity 100.

	Per 100		Per 100
[Ma]yfort No. 4 .	23/-	Panatelas (Long Thin Cigars) .	15/-
[Havan]as (Long Thin [C]igars) .	16/-	*Postage the same as for Tobacco.*	

TOBACCO

BY PARCELS POST

	Per lb.		Per lb.
[May]fort—Mild .	6/-	Cake Tobacco for the Troops (dark) .	1/9
,, Medium .	5/6		
[Smo]king Mixture No. 1	5/6	Cake Tobacco for the	

PROVISION BOX No.

FOR SHIPMENT
For 6 to 8 Officers.

2 1-lb Tins English Meat (Pressed Beef, Sliced Ham, etc.)	1 1-lb Tin Ideal M[ilk]
	1 lb Chocolate (ext[ra])
3 4-oz Tins Potted Meats (various)	1 Tin Fortnum & M[ason]
	1 Castor Table Sal[t]
2 No. 1 Tins Biscuits (various)	1 Plum Pudding
1 Tin (6) Soup Squares ,,	4 Export Candles
1 ½-lb Tin Dorset Butter	1 Tin Safety Match[es]
1 ½-lb Tin Cheese (Cheddar, Gruyère, etc.)	2 Cakes Toilet Soa[p]
	1 Combined Tin O[pener]
1 ¼-lb Tin Tea	Corkscrew
1 1-lb Tin Loaf Sugar	1 Deal Box comp[lete]
	Padlock and Ke[y]

Measurement of Box 18 in. by 10 in. by 10 in[ches]

Gross Weight 28 lbs.

Price £1

PROVISION BOX No. 1

FOR SHIPMENT
For 6 to 8 Officers.

2 1-lb Tins Oxford Sausages	1 1-lb Tin Ideal Mi[lk]
2 1-lb Tins English Meat (Pressed Beef, Sliced Ham, etc.)	1 Tin Fortnum & Ma[son]
	1 lb Chocolate (Extr[a])
3 4-oz Tins Potted Meats (various kinds)	1 Plum Pudding
	1 Castor Table Salt
1 Bottle Worcester Sauce	50 Finest Turkish C[igarettes]
2 No. 2 Tins Biscuits (various)	2 ½-lb Tins Smoking [Mixture]
1 Tin (6) Soup Squares ,,	4 Export Candles, e[tc.]
1 ½-lb Dorset Butter	1 Tin Safety Matche[s]
	2 Cakes Toilet Soa[p]

WW2

The Officers' Department once more saw distinguished service. As well as comestibles it dealt in insect powder, exotic cigarettes and anything else the modern soldier might require, such as an EPNS tip for a bayonet (so much more elegant for spreading one's Gentleman's Relish at El Alamein) and the "Spork", the combination knife-and fork which, naturally, came silver-plated.

Arbiters of decorum even in wartime, the company also patented the "Fortknee', a short stocking to cover the knees and lower thighs of lady drivers in the services.

The Military this Millennium

Captain Lipton was in a fix. In May 2006 his troops were at their base in Basra but lacked decent tea. As he put it: "The mess hall provides the usual "get you through" products but these fall far short in the quality zone". How do we know? Because, aware of Fortnum's track record in supporting the British forces overseas, he requested urgent assistance. We didn't stew over the issue for long, despatching enough tins of Royal Blend to see them through their next tour in Afghanistan. How could we refuse tea to a man with such a name?

Fortnum & Mason's
(Original Note heading in the 18th Century)

GROCERY, TEA & SPICE WAREHOUSE.
— Importers of Foreign Fruits —
& Dealers in English & Foreign Honey
183, **PICCADILLY**, nearly opposite **ALBANY.**

Fortnum & Tea

From our foundation in 1707 Fortnum's imported tea and sold it to anyone who asked, a pioneering idea at a time when tea was generally confined to the aristocracy. Three centuries later it's even more important to the realm and, it must be said, to Fortnum's. We sell more tea than ever, to more countries than before (including the very ones who started the whole thing brewing).

Still very much a pioneering enterprise, we also offer more varieties from more countries than ever. We've always been the place to come for the season's first arrivals and more countries means more seasons to enjoy. Tea's map has expanded in recent years and our range is wider and deeper than ever. We're all for innovation: after all, it's what's kept us on top of things for all this while. That and a regular tipple of tip-top tea. Chin-chin!

Dr. Johnson and Mrs. Thrale over tea and cakes.
We were an old-established firm even in those days

English Tea Ahoy

Who'd have thought it? More than a century after the famous tea clipper races shrank the ocean to arrive at Scilly in four choppy months, we discover that terrific tea is now available a mere day or two's ride from Piccadilly. Tucked away on the banks of the River Fal in Cornwall is the Tregothnan Estate, Home of Lord Falmouth's family since 1335. Secretly developed over the last eight years and heralded as the "Next Darjeeling", the perfected tea has become in short order one of the world's most sought-after. How fitting that the first truly English tea is now available from Fortnum & Mason.

Boston Tea Party

It's not on record who supplied the tea in 1773, but it was probably not us: none of ours do at all well with salt water. Since Independence, though, our American cousins have been among our most loyal customers.

Plum Puddings

Christmas isn't Christmas without plum pudding, of which the alpha and omega come from Fortnum & Mason. Originally one's cook would create one's own house style, with Fortnum's essential only to supply the very best of ingredients. Some demand for ready-cooked puddings came for Victorian picnics (at Christmas? Hardy souls!) but it was the expatriate community that drove the real growth. After 1918 the domestic market for ready-made puddings grew apace. In December 1923, noted that there was an unusually heavy demand for plum puddings at Fortnum & Mason, "...the reason being the domestic servant difficulty." From then on, the institution that is the Fortnum & Mason Christmas pudding was assured, and shopping columns of newspapers and magazine invariably mentioned the superior nature, and ancient recipe, of the Fortnum & Mason pudding.

The Fortnum & Mason plum pudding is different from that found elsewhere. It has more fruit, more brandy, more subtle spicing. It cannot be mistaken for another brand. For that reason, the recipe (guarded over many generations) is kept under lock and key in the company archive. That doesn't stop us innovating, even if progress is sometimes backwards: our latest King George pudding uses a Georgian recipe involving real beef suet for a stouter body, much like the eponymous gourmand himself (by which one may gather that we mean the Fourth).

Pies

Within a few years of its foundation, Fortnum & Mason was renowned for its ready-cooked food. Top of the list was the raised pie. Charles Dickens was a particular fan of our Yorkshire pies, sending his butler off to Piccadilly whenever he finished a novel.

Fortnum & Mason pies are central to a political anecdote. After the stormy passage of the 1867 Electoral Reform Act, Prime Minister Benjamin Disraeli called in at the Carlton Club to great acclaim from his fellow conservatives. They pressed him to stay and dine with them, but he went home to his wife, who recalled,

Dizzy came home to me: I had got him a raised pie from Fortnum & Mason's and a bottle of champagne and he ate half the pie and drank all the champagne and then he said; "Why, my dear, you are more like a mistress than a wife".

Chagrined Seagull being refused admittance to a Fortnum & Mason Game Pie

Good & Curious Honey

It stands to reason that a company founded on the recycling of beeswax should know a thing or two about honey. From its inception, Fortnum & Mason has sought the best and greatest variety of honeys. At the Great Exhibition of 1851, its display of various honeys was praised as, *"… good and curious, and well worthy of attention; it is the result of much pains to illustrate this branch of trade."*

Not only did Fortnum & Mason offer the greatest variety of honeys, but it boasted from the Victorian period that – unlike its competitors – the honey was extracted from their improved top hives *without killing the bees*. This not only meant that the honey was produced in a humane way, but that the survival of the hives ensured consistency of product. Not content with relying on ages-old techniques, Fortnum & Mason experimented with honey. Leigh Hunt, a noted journalist, described how people came to Piccadilly especially to see a display of rose coloured honey in the shop windows. It was of great beauty and delicacy, with a virgin comb which was almost white, the honey being limpid and the colour of pale redcurrant jelly. The secret production was not revealed, except that it was the result of artificial feeding. In January 1871, the company presented a jar of this honey to the Food Department of the South Kensington Museum.

Fortnum's Rooftop Bees

The tale of Fortnum's bees began with the observation that within a three-mile radius of Piccadilly lay a variety of flora unequalled in the countryside. Then came the suggestion that honey from local pollen is the most effective combatant of hay fever. There was only one thing for it: to the drawing-board!

Plans approved, we set to work on the roof of our venerable edifice. The entrances to our stately Eau de Nil hives emulate Georgian triumphal arches: after all, ours are no humdrum bumblers. The bees' elevated address affords spectacular views of three cathedrals and two seats of government while nearby nectar is found at St James's and Buckingham Palaces, plentiful parks, squares, gardens and window boxes. It is not known whether they ever venture south of the river.

Wine

Until the 1940s, the cellarmen at Fortnum & Mason bottled the precious liquid in the cool wine vault deep under Duke Street, where customers (at no extra charge) could leave their prized stocks until required.

Port, Superior Claret, Sherry and Marsala came by the Pipe, Hogshead, Quarter Cask and Gallon. Malmsey, however, was sold by the Quart.

In those far-off days the cellar sold only the finest traditional wines from France, Germany, Spain and Portugal. Liqueurs (especially cherry brandy) were hugely popular among the Victorians and Edwardians. "Exotics" included Crèmes de Noyeau, Vanille, Thé, Rose, Moribolanti, Barbados and Parfait d'Amour. Perhaps the effects of Extract d'Absynthe boosted the sales of Milk Punch and Eau Vulneraive Suisse, otherwise known as "Stomachic Liqueur".

Today, wines from around the globe (and increasingly from England) are purveyed by cellarmen every bit as knowledgeable and distinguished as their predecessors – as evidenced by the award of "London's Best Wine List" as soon as our 1707 Wine Bar opened its doors to a thirsty public.

Young Mr Heinz

Such authority made us the obvious first stop for a young entrepreneur in 1866 lugging five cases of samples from the USA. Recognising a future staple we took them all, introducing the mighty baked bean to Britain for the first time: another entry in our ever-expanding list of gastronomic firsts.

The Wine Crypt Over page: Heinz 57 in 1957

DEMONSTRATION BY H.J. HEINZ "57"

ORANGE JUICE 2/-

TOMATO CHUTNEY 3/-

HEINZ SOUPS 10½ & 1/3

MR. HEINZ ARRIVES 1886 AT FORTNUM MASON

A Golden Day

One day in 1886 a man from far away Pittsburgh stepped from a hansom cab outside the famous store of Fortnum and Mason in Piccadilly.

He was HENRY J. HEINZ the founder of the now world famous house which had been established seventeen years earlier in 1869.

Here at his first call, he opened and sampled five cases of his products and because of their quality and flavour Fortnum and Mason bought them all.

Encouraged by this reception HENRY J. HEINZ went on to build up a wonderful business in Great Britain where its continued development is in notable tribute to the superlative quality of The 57 Varieties.

Chocolate

For decades chocolate was made by hand at 181 Piccadilly. Memories of those days can still be found:

"...if you are interested and ask your very polite assistant, [the principal shopman] will no doubt be pleased to take you up to the sixth floor to see the white-overalled girls making, decorating and packing the chocolates which are so particularly delicious because no synthetic flavourings whatever are used in them."

Dr Sloane, I Presume

Dr Hans Sloane, physician to Queen Anne and enthusiastic amateur botanist, had encountered the cocoa bean while on tour in the West Indies. He developed a recipe for drinking chocolate "the English way" that he patented and promoted as a healthy alternative to alcohol. In the eighteenth and nineteenth centuries, Fortnum & Mason sold chocolate for drinking (and occasionally cooking) under Sloane's patent. French chocolate for invalids was imported from the mid nineteenth century, and French bonbons became increasingly popular as the century drew to a close. It was not until the 1920s that Fortnum & Mason had the space – and the expert, one William Pain – to create its own chocolate factory. After an interlude in Brewer Street, production returned to Piccadilly where it remained until the 1980s. These days our signature chocolates are still being made by the company set up by Mr Pain.

Your Crackers, m'Lady

Since Tom Smith first put the snap in a decorated cardboard tube, Fortnum & Mason has sold crackers. By the 1920s we were justly famous for spectacular specimens. Let's pull a few.

Pulling Crackers

Pulling crackers came in the shape of turkeys, pastries, bottles of champagne, barrels of beer, fish, fruit, Christmas cakes and even a large slice of wedding cake, evidence that they weren't confined to Christmas. In 1933 we introduced crackers for bachelor parties, with suitable racy contents. There were also giant pulling crackers, designed as tug-of war items (up to 6 feet long!) for parties.

Standing Crackers

Life-size figures with strings – pull the strings, the figure explodes, showering everyone with smaller crackers. The range changed over the years to cover beefeaters, guardsmen, gnomes, giant frogs and pigs. One year featured a giant figure of the devil with electric eyes that lit up. Father Christmas, red indians, pirates, princesses, princes and clowns all stood to attention over the years, as did life-sized crackers of the most popular British stage and screen personalities.

Table Crackers

A giant model of The Golden Hind that explodes when each guest tugs an anchor? Naturally, madam. How about Santa's sleigh, The Fairy Queen on hers, or Cinderella's slippers? For weddings there were figures of a bride and a groom for the table, and a sweep who showered the table with crackers for each guest. Given the number of crackers with a hunting scene, Fortnum's obviously sold many to Hunt Ball organisers. A giant Christmas pudding with a lit-up nose was sold for several years, as was a giant pumpkin that scattered toys everywhere. Our favourite may be the windmill with actual turning blades, though it faces stiff competition from the galleon in full sail and… ooh, dozens more.

ℭ NEW CRACKERS

in COVEYS, COHORTS, LEGIONS and
LARGE NUMBERS
such as cause
AMAZEMENT & FURIOUS HAPPINESS
to ALL BEHOLDERS, collected in
℘ Our New Cracker Department ꝫ

WE have had such a scene with our gifted Christmas Cracker Expert! He demanded a whole department to display his marvellous crackers. As he had already stabbed one Director we consented—these talented people *are* difficile.

¶ The New Cracker Department is at the corner of Fortnum & Mason's, the Duke St.–Jermyn St. corner.

¶ A veritable house of crackers. Dazzling mountains of them. Crackers you cannot help rooting amongst because you continually find something new. How we laughed when we saw the real Japanese ones we import from Osaka. Inside the third one we found . . . . . . but we mustn't tell before Christmas—anyhow, we *roared*. We shall be really upset if you do not see them. Christmas without such crackers as ours is unthinkable.

¶ Here is a map to show you the way. It is drawn by our hydrographer who has been in the firm since its foundation in 1710. We call him "H" for short

FORTNUM & MASON   182 PICCADILLY w

The bend   The tension   The Split

Courtesy – the assistant who bowed once too often

Fortnum & Service

While inventing a new type of retail environment for a new type of customer, Fortnum's pioneered a fresh brand of service that remains a unique hallmark. Its most recognisable traits are profound product knowledge rendered with exquisite courtesy. As one commentator remarked in 1925:

"It is so nice to be treated like a Duchess while one is buying a pound of coffee."

As long as the customer is female, we heartily agree.

The Maharaja Department

Another opportunity to go the extra few thousand miles came in 1935 with the Jubilee of King George V. The even drew so many princes and potentates from all corners of the Empire that Fortnum & Mason, having long imported the best from all the continents, created a special department to accommodate their dietary requirements. To whom else might one possibly have turned?

Personal service at Fortnum's in 1958

The Fortnum & Mason Postal Service

Until the General Post Office came into being, the business of sending and receiving mail was open to anyone - and Fortnum's grasped the opportunity. It had letterboxes for paid and unpaid letters which were picked up six times a day (in the days before stamps the recipient usually picked up the bill). Soldiers and sailors, already among the company's best customers, received a discount. The arrangement drew all sorts of traffic to the store to be tempted by the already magnificent window and interior displays. This arrangement lasted until 1839, when the GPO was founded – a year before the Penny Black with its bust of a youthful Victoria.

Cowes

In July 1933 Fortnum & Mason branched out, opening up a shop in the Isle of Wight for Cowes Week. The shop, supplied from London by 'plane and "fast motor-vans," had its own motorboat which delivered goods free of charge to yachts taking part in the regatta.

Dick Turpin stole our Beef Tea to enable him to ride to York
(we were within an ace of catching him that night)

Living Above the Shop

In the 18th and 19th centuries, unmarried members of staff (all male, naturally) lived at 181 Piccadilly – as did members of the Fortnum family. They were on hand to supply a needy customer with calves' foot jelly or strengthening port at any time of the night. Staff tended to stay – it was not unusual for clerks or shopmen to work at "The Great House" all their working lives, referring to themselves as part of the Fortnum Family. In the 1920s and 1930s the Fortnum & Mason advertisers built on this, creating a mythical Fortnum's where all the staff lived in under a quasi-military regime. The buyers and supervisors were the sergeant majors, constantly exasperated by the antics and the effervescence of the junior other ranks. Female employees (always beautiful, virginal and demure) took part in ancient ceremonies to celebrate venerable cheeses, the arrival of foie gras and the season's fruits. How magical.

Setting Pâtés to music at Fortnum's

Staff Legends

Other members of staff live on in legend. For example, Gaius Backholer was due to retire in 1939 after nearly fifty years' service, but stayed on to serve throughout the Second World War. When he finally retired in 1946, The Princess Royal called at the shop to say a personal farewell.

Joyce Wethered, women's amateur golfing champion, worked at the store as golfing consultant in the 1930s. Fortnum's was immensely proud of its recruit, promising that Miss Wethered *"...is always in Fortnum's sports department and glad to help you with advice on golfing matters. As you doubtless know, she recently returned from a brilliantly successful golfing tour in Canada and the United States."*

Marcel Boulestin

Noted designer, restaurateur and cookery writer Marcel Boulestin began writing cookery books in 1923. *Simple French Cooking for English Homes* was an instant hit with the postwar generation of families who no longer had a resident Cook. Over the next fifteen years he produced a dozen volumes taking the mystery out of Gallic cooking and opened a hugely successful restaurant in Covent Garden. Fortnum & Mason spotted him early and persuaded him to run what turned out to be wildly popular cookery courses at Piccadilly, where hatted and fur-decked ladies learned the mysteries of the perfect Veal Marengo.

Top: Miss Joyce Wethered, Fortnum's golfing consultant, 1933
Bottom: Marcel Boulestin, the "famous master of cooking", 1935

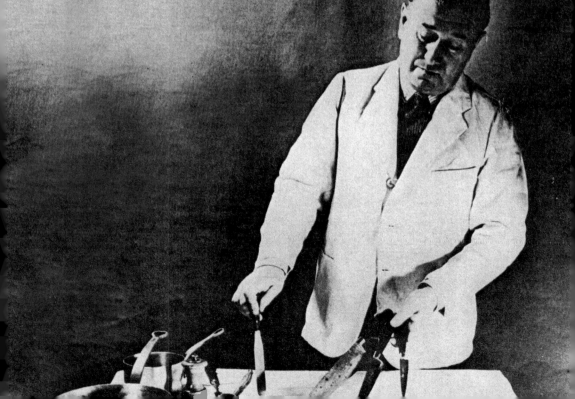

Arthur Lunn

The most celebrated proponent of the Fortnum ethos was Arthur Lunn. Born in 1897, the year of Victoria's Diamond Jubilee, he worked at Piccadilly from 1933 until 1990.

Mr. Lunn famously took a course in Pelmanism to help him remember all of his customers' names, addresses and culinary preferences. He cultivated a large and distinguished clientele including the crowned heads of Europe and Hollywood's own royalty – and as his sense of discretion was impeccable, many refused to be served by anyone else. As Mr Lunn observed, "When someone asks for me by name, that's my repayment and my reward." Ever the enlightened employer, however, Fortnum's insisted on paying him a respectable salary as well.

Mr Fortnum's Fortune

Fortnum & Mason has always understood that if shopping here is to remain a unique pleasure, our greatest assets need looking after. The Fortnum family and their descendents had a close relationship with their small staff. In 1846 one of the partners, Richard Fortnum, left £1500 (about £50,000 today) to the Piccadilly staff who had served him so faithfully and so well. Twenty years later, some of the sixty members of staff at Fortnum & Mason were among the founders of The Grocers' Assistants' Provident Association, designed to improve the social conditions of assistants in the grocery trade. In this they were fully supported by their employers.

Dining in Piccadilly

For many, the first encounter with Fortnum & Mason is being taken out to eat, often by a relative other than one's parent. The Knickerbocker Glory often plays a central role alongside Godparent, Aunt or anyone better equipped to spoil than plain old Mater and Pater.

Once acquired, the habit tends to stay: often breakfast or a pre-theatre meal at the The Fountain restaurant, lunch at the Gallery before braving the Royal Academy Summer Exhibition or a champagne afternoon tea in the quiet luxury of the St James's on the 4th.

However, eating at Fortnum's is itself a relatively young phenomenon. The first eating area for customers was opened in 1930 when the restaurant (later the Patio) served morning coffee, light lunches and afternoon cups of tea to ladies up from the country. The quality of the cooking and service, combined with the irresistibility of the cake and chocolate counters on the same mezzanine floor, caused a stir among newspaper shopping correspondents. It soon became *the* place to be seen in Mayfair.

Just as post-War rationing was finally coming to an end, Fortnum's launched a restaurant named for the real American soda fountain in the middle of the floor, but what really put The Fountain on the map was the iconic Knickerbocker Glory. After nearly 15 years of sugar rationing these mountains of ice cream, fruit, nuts, whipped cream and glacé fruit made sure that children of all ages came back again and again.

These days The Fountain is a sober haven of respectability while its legacy lives on in The Parlour, our brand new First Floor restaurant that aims to fill the same "first outing" brief as its predecessor. The St James's Restaurant is still an elegant oasis of old-fashioned service while the Wine Bar was winning awards from its opening. All of this means Fortnum's is able to serve more people under one roof as pretty much anywhere in London. It's all quite some way from brunch at The Buttery.

First row: St James's Restaurant, 1973
Second row left: Knickerbocker Glorious; The Fountain, 1955 *Second row right:* The Buttery, c1960
Third row left: The Patio from the Buttery, c1960 *Third row right:* The last spoonful; the Buttery, 1955

Everest & Other Expeditions

Fortnum's is the only store to have had a department dedicated to "Expeditions", at a time when huge consignments of home comforts - right down to such essentials as butter knives and sauce boats - accompanied the English into the heart of Africa and up the Himalayas. The 1922 Everest expedition, for example, simply couldn't start without 60 tins of quail in foie gras and four dozen bottles of champagne (the appropriately-named Montebello 1915).

The 1933 team, including a young Tensing Norgay, was dismayed to find several of the delicacies replaced by stones, presumably by inquisitive customs officers. Only the Stiltons remained, their covers pierced but the fragrant contents, clearly not to the Nepalese nose, left untouched.

In warmer climes Howard Carter's Tutankhamun expedition used Fortnum's wine boxes to help catalogue the rare antiquities, including a statue of the boy-king as Aten, the Sun: representing tacit approval from yet another monarch.

What use-by-date?

Fortnum & Mason supplied provisions to Sir John Franklin on his doomed expedition to the Arctic in 1845, and also supplied crates of tinned foods for Lady Franklin, for her many attempts to find her missing husband. Several tins of meat and fruit have been recovered from these expeditions, and, when opened were 'found to be perfectly packed, and without any sign of putrefaction."

Top: A handshake of friendship and a Fortnum's hamper;
the Ascend the Nile Expedition, the endeavour to find the source of the Nile, 2005.
Bottom: Fortnum & Mason Tea Tin buried on a summit of Mt Fettes, New Zealand, 1995

Celebrating our 250th Birthday, 1957

Celebrations

Fortnum & Mason lives in the heart of the West End, close to palaces, the royal parks and the Houses of Parliament. It has witnessed many celebrations over the centuries. Situated on the route for most of the Coronation processions over the past three centuries, the shop always 'dressed up' for such occasions. In 1953 the shopfront sprouted scaffolding, bunting and seating to allow the privileged few customers a perfect view of the procession. Being Fortnum's customers, of course, each was supplied with a picnic to enjoy during the long day, and the Spanish Bar stayed open for the spectators. Crowds along the route could also order the special Coronation hamper, ready for collection at Piccadilly early on the morning of the ceremony. The catering staff were busy that day, for it was Fortnum & Mason who also supplied the Coronation Banquet that evening.

Above: The Jubilee – Unrehearsed Incident
Left: Fortnum & Mason decorated for the Coronation of Queen Elizabeth II, 1953

BY APPOINTMENT
TO HER MAJESTY QUEEN ELIZABETH II
GROCERS & PROVISION MERCHANTS
FORTNUM & MASON PLC. LONDON

BY APPOINTMENT
TO H.R.H. THE PRINCE OF WALES
TEA MERCHANTS AND GROCERS
FORTNUM & MASON PLC. LONDON

Royal Warrants

As befits a company with its origins in royal service, Fortnum & Mason has enjoyed the enthusiastic patronage of successive monarchs. Today's warrants relate to grocery and provisions, but in the 19th and early 20th century we held several as oilmen and tea dealers. In 1867 we became the proud possessors of a royal warrant as 'furnishers to the establishment' of Queen Victoria's eldest daughter, the Crown Princess of Prussia, Princess Royal of Great Britain and Ireland.

The most exotic warrant in our collection was issued in 1923 by Taffari Makonen, heir apparent to the Throne of Ethiopia. He is better remembered today as Emperor Haile Selasse, the Lion of Judah – whose one and only visit to Britain began and ended on the tarmac at Heathrow, so overawed was he by the size of the welcoming crowds. Far safer, he decided, to let England come to him – in the shape of regular orders from Fortnum's.

Detail from Haile Selasse Warrant, 1923

American's first introduction to bread sauce

Madison Avenue

In April 1931 Fortnum & Mason opened up a seven-story building on New York's Madison Avenue, based on the design of the Piccadilly building and luxuriously furnished to resemble a more prosperous twin of its Piccadilly counterpart. Fortnum & Mason Incorporated was launched with the express intention of developing the business in Fortnum & Mason products in America, mainly because the London store had enjoyed ever-increasing American business throughout the 1920s. It was very consciously British, selling British-made goods, (especially women's country clothes and footwear) and selling the idea of a British lifestyle that was familiar to the Americans through films and the works of P.G.Wodehouse. Adverts were taken out in magazines patronised by the elite of East-coast America, though sadly the wine department – where the company had hoped to do well – was refused permission to advertise either in print or on the radio.

Members of the Fortnum's board zigzagged across the Atlantic on Cunard and White Star liners to keep the company on track, and there was healthy competition among the buyers at Piccadilly for secondments to Manhattan. In the time between conception and execution, however the Depression had begun to bite, making it a star that burned brightly but all too briefly.

697-699 Madison Avenue, New York, 1931

The Weston Family

In 1951 the "Canadian Prince of Industry" acquired control of the company's reins. Though he had extensive interests in other areas, most notably the manufacture of millions' daily bread and the invention of that all-round success the Wagon Wheel, Fortnum's became the jewel in his empire's crown.

Symbolically, at least. Garfield Weston told reporters at London Airport that "The acquisition will not give me another thousand a year income." Despite this perhaps mischievous aside, he took a personal interest and kept it separate from his other businesses, investing in Fortnum's future in a way that recognised its two greatest assets: 181 Piccadilly and the staff who keep it at the very top of the pile.

By the date of the 250th anniversary in 1957 his innovations included cash registers with no bells and a broadened product base to include clothing, antiques and the opening of a soda fountain and hairdressing salon.

Garfield Weston's descendants are very much still in control today, continuing a tradition established by the founders: active personal interest from the very top, in an establishment cherished as unique. The last Fortnum gave way to Colonel Wyld after almost 200 years and half a century later came the Weston family, ensuring that our stately galleon has always had a firm hand on the tiller.

In an offbeat homage to the pioneering Weston, the latest flavour in Fortnum's new ice-cream Parlour goes by the name of Rota Plaustri and tastes, as any schoolboy should be able to tell you, of Wagon Wheel.

Fortnum's Famous Fans

While today's celebrated faces may be assured of utmost discretion when shopping with us, we believe it fair to mention a few of our more famous patrons from the past.

Monarchs

From Queen Anne onwards, our Royal connections have never been severed. Edward VII enjoyed daily orders when living at Marlborough House as Prince of Wales while Edward VIII was sent kippers and marmalade in France while waiting to get married to Mrs Simpson.

Other Notables

Rosa Lewis, "Queen of Cooks, Duchess of Duke Street" and proprietor of the Cavendish hotel, was naturally an account holder and came every day - often to the invisible dismay of our long-suffering staff.

Disraeli (pies and champagne) and Gladstone (sugar and tea) found Fortnum's one thing they could agree on. Winston Churchill came for his own-label champagne and would often leave with Dundee cake as well.

Charles Dickens adored our pies and ham, John Betjeman our tea. As for George Bernard Shaw, we're not George Bernard sure - though confident he would have avoided the meat counter.

Marlene Dietrich fell in love again and again with our shoes while Robert Morley took our fun invalid boxes on his regular hospital visits but made sure to add champagne.

Mother Teresa of Calcutta had an easy task of persuading us to put on Christmas breakfast for London's homeless, and… enough.

If we were the sort of store to tell more, there's lots more we could tell.

Into Our Fourth Century

Who knows what further far-flung fans Fortnum's will find as the fledgling millennium spreads it's wings and flies into the future?

Thanks to technology our reach is now wider than ever, which is in perfect tune with the pioneering spirit that drove our earliest enterprises. Our core values of courtesy and excellence, though, have not changed any more than the recipe for King George Plum Pudding.

Fortnum & Mason goes wwworldwide

In 1998 Fortnum & Mason went truly global by extending its reach into the digital universe. The first online store launched with just hampers - but there were 50 of them. Soon the range grew to include classic gifts from our Food Hall and by the turn of the millennium the site featured over 800 products.

The current site has both UK and US versions and brings the spirit of entertainment and celebration alive on every page.

Bricks & Mortar

181 Piccadilly is now totally enlightened and refurbished, awash with new resatuants and vibrant departments.

We've gone forth and we've multiplied: at the time of writing we have thirteen stores in Japan and a thriving American operation.

We're still breaking new ground: 2007 saw our first garden at Chelsea win a Gold award.

Who can tell what lies just up ahead?

Left: The Fortnum & Mason beehives at Chelsea
Right: The Atrium, 2006

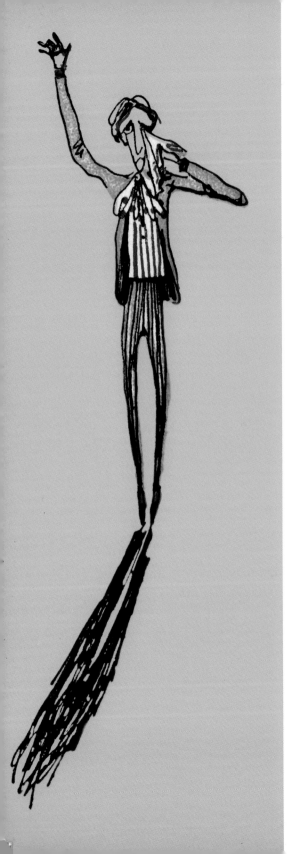

Picture Credits

Cover Illustration – Ian Bilbey
Page 15 – Advertisements: Harpers
Page 63 – Personal service at
Fortnum's: George Miles
Page 69 – Joyce Wethered:
National Trust. Marcel Boulestin:
Michael Parkin
Page 75 – Mt Fettes, New Zealand:
A V Macleod Murray
Page 85 – The Queen Mother:
Associated Press; Charles Dickens:
Bridgeman Art; Rosa Lewis: courtesy
of the Cavendish Hotel; Sir Winston
Churchill: Mary Evans Picture Library

© Fortnum & Mason plc 2007

Graphic Designer Lizzie Ballantyne
Honorary Archivist Dr Andrea Duncan
Copy Writer Tim Lawler
Editor Yvonne Isherwood

Made and printed in England
by Norwich Colour Print

Published by Fortnum & Mason plc
181 Piccadilly, London
W1A 1ER England
www.fortnumandmason.co.uk

ISBN 978-0-9556693-0-9

FORTNUM & MASON
PICCADILLY SINCE 1707